Moving From Vision to Reality

Happy About Fulfilling Your True Purpose

By Cyril Rayan

HappyAbout.info

21265 Stevens Creek Blvd.
Suite 205
Cupertino, CA 95014

Moving From Vision to Reality: Happy About Fulfilling Your True Purpose

First Printing: April 27, 2007
Paperback ISBN: 1-60005-047-6
Place of Publication: Silicon Valley, California, USA
Library of Congress Number: 2007926685

eBook ISBN: 1-60005-048-4

Trademarks

Warning and Disclaimer

Praise for Moving From Vision to Reality (from the back cover)

"Well-written, easy to read and filled with deep understanding. This book is a must for anyone interested in leadership or starting a company. I contemplated writing a similar book, but felt God had something else in mind for me. Now, I know why: Rayan nailed the concept of leadership God's way and by the way, the best way for success."
Ken Eldred, Entrepreneur and Author

"Cyril Rayan is passionate about helping others discover their destiny. His latest work; 'Moving From Vision to Reality' should be placed in the hands of all those wanting to become great leaders for the Kingdom and for Kingdom business."
Rich Marshall, Author and Leadership Coach

"Cyril Rayan has produced an excellent volume that clearly articulates the process between catching a vision and developing the plan of action for achieving the purposes of the vision. The field of literature on Leadership is filled with wide-ranging definitions, but very few provide the tools for crafting and motivating a working team to help the organization arrive at reality and achievement. Rayan has generously contributed to the Leadership Field with 'Moving From Vision to Reality', and I highly recommend this book to everyone who cares about competent leadership, resourceful vision casting, and successful organization performance!"
Máximo Rossi, Jr., Ph.D., President, Bethany University, Scotts Valley, California

"The book is by all means a researched expository which is a must read for anyone aspiring to be a visionary leader in any sector. It's a book that I wholeheartedly endorse and recommend to anyone desiring to chart out an emulable destiny! Read this book and you will treasure the jewels of wisdom in it."
Bishop Pius Muiru, Founder& President Maximum Miracle Center, Kenya

Additional Praise for Moving From Vision to Reality

"This book gives the importance of vision and purpose and the essential ingredients to implement them well. It applies both the biblical and business principles with practical experience and is a easy and good reading for everyone"
Isaac Sundarajan, CEO, Codenomicon

"The book 'Moving From Vision to Reality', integrates Biblical leaders and truths of scripture with leadership principles. In addition, it draws from many of history's finest leaders to underscore and focus leadership theory and practice. The material is well organized and presented with questions at the end of each chapter to assist the reader in personal application or for usage in small study groups. It is a practical book, which the reader will find helpful for self-discovery in leadership."
Bryce Jessup, President, William Jessup University, Rocklin, California

"There are those who think that turning vision into reality involves self-effort, will power and sacrifice. Others think that it is pure fate where they have no part to play - God chooses some for greatness and others for the ordinary. In this practical study, Cyril Rayan shows us the truth by pointing us to God from whom our purpose comes and to ourselves from whom the decision to act must arise."
Guy Tcheau, CEO & President, Buildfolio, Inc., Singapore

"Cyril Rayan notes in 'Moving From Vision to Reality' that all of us are in leadership positions from time to time. Many of us, however, fail to fulfill our vision for leadership. Rayan offers proven, practical advice on how to fulfill our God-given purpose and to make our vision a reality. I recommend it for everyone who has a desire to lead effectively."
Skip Vaccarello, Management Consultant and Executive Coach

"'Moving From Vision to Reality' leads the reader to embrace a higher vision and then follow the calling… A modern day 'Think & Grow Rich'"
Joe Pelayo, Author of: Work Your Network!

"'Moving From Vision to Reality' is a book that seeks to give the leader of today a strong grasp of the essential truths of leadership from both a spiritual and practical perspective. The book demonstrates strong research and insights gleaned both from practical life experience and research. Having the privilege of knowing the Author and having worked with him, I can attest to his passion and desire to help emerging leaders to develop and achieve a life vision. This is a book that needs to be read and reflected on and digested well, it will stir up the vision within you."
Sr. Pastor Dan Griffiths, North Valley Christian Fellowship

Publisher

- Mitchell Levy, http://www.happyabout.info/

Cover Designer

- Cate Calson, http://www.calsongraphics.com/

Chief Editor

- Frank Mitchell, www.kingdomauthor.com

Dedication

To my wife and best friend, Jemima, and our children, Hannah and Joshua.

To my parents, Ignatius and Rani Rayan. They encourage me, believe in me, advise me, mentor me and pray for me.

Cyril Rayan
San Jose, California

Acknowledgements

I feel a deep sense of gratitude to my wonderful wife, Jemima, who is my spiritual mentor and who supports me and works together with me in running with the vision that the Lord has given us.

I would like to acknowledge Joseph Manoharan, who is a good friend and who was my first spiritual mentor. It was he, who invited me to go to a Myles Munroe meeting in 1995, which changed my life. It was in that meeting that I began to understand the concepts of purpose, potential, and vision.

I would also like to acknowledge Frank Mitchell, a wonderful friend whose time was much appreciated in terms of helping me edit this book and refine it.

I appreciate Jill Okamura, a good friend who has also spent time editing this book and who also helped with the layout and bibliography.

I am grateful to Bob Grandey and Joseph Childs for having given me the opportunity to teach leadership courses at William Jessup University and Bethany University (respectively). Teaching has definitely helped me gain more insights on this topic.

I also want to thank Mary Sundararaj of Carmel Web Designs for helping design the graphics for this book. I admire her patience and spirit of excellence.

I am thankful to Mitchell Levy who is the CEO of Happy About, publisher of this book for believing in me and for the opportunity to work together to publish my first book.

Last but not least, I was happy to work with Lynda Holland, one of my students at Bethany, who introduced me to the morale study she took in her workplace. Some data from that study has been incorporated into the text.

A Message From Happy About®

Thank you for your purchase of this Happy About book. It is available online at http://happyabout.info/myfaith/vision2reality.php or at other online and physical bookstores.

- Please contact us for quantity discounts at sales@happyabout.info
- If you want to be informed by e-mail of upcoming Happy About® books, please e-mail bookupdate@happyabout.info

Happy About is interested in you if you are an author who would like to submit a non-fiction book proposal or a corporation that would like to have a book written for you. Please contact us by e-mail editorial@happyabout.info or phone (1-408-257-3000).

Other Happy About books available include:

- Happy About My Christian Faith
  http://happyabout.info/myfaith/mychristianfaith.php
- Climbing the Ladder of Business Inteligence:
  http://happyabout.info/climbing-ladder.php
- Overcoming Inventoritis:
  http://happyabout.info/overcoming-inventoritis.php
- Happy About People-to-People Lending With Prosper.com:
  http://happyabout.info/prosper/
- Happy About Online Networking:
  http://happyabout.info/onlinenetworking.php
- Happy About Apartment Management:
  http://happyabout.info/apartment-management.php
- Confessions of a Resilient Entrepreneur:
  http://happyabout.info/confessions-entrepreneur.php
- Memoirs of the Money Lady:
  http://happyabout.info/memoirs-money-lady.php
- 30-Day Bootcamp: Your Ultimate Life Makeover:
  http://happyabout.info/30daybootcamp/life-makeover.php
- The Business Rule Revolution:
  http://happyabout.info/business-rule-revolution.php
- Happy About Global Software Test Automation:
  http://happyabout.info/globalswtestautomation.php
- Happy About Joint Venturing:
  http://happyabout.info/jointventuring.php
- Happy About LinkedIn for Recruiting:
  http://happyabout.info/linkedin4recruiting.php
- Happy About Website Payments with PayPal
  http://happyabout.info/paypal.php

C o n t e n t s

Introduction

The reason I decided to write this book is that I often hear visions and dreams from many people around me, but do not see them being implemented or even acted upon. This led me to ponder on what it takes for a vision to become a reality and why so few really venture into acting upon their vision. I am optimistic that after thorough reading and comprehension, this book will allow more people to be inspired to act upon their vision; hopefully making the world we live in a better one. This book brings together the elements needed to take your vision and make it a reality.

There are seven steps, which are necessary to move from vision to reality. Some of the steps are addressed in one particular chapter while others are addressed in multiple chapters. At the end of each chapter, there are workbook exercises that contain key summary points and space for you to make notations in the book. These have been established to help reinforce the key message of each chapter. There are also questions to help apply what you learned to your personal life.

The Seven Steps

Step 1: Find your Purpose and Catch the Vision
Step 2: Decide to Act and Write the Vision
Step 3: Build a Team to Accomplish the Vision
Step 4: Manage the Team & Foster Innovation
Step 5: Believe in the Vision
Step 6: Run with the Vision
Step 7: Hang on to the Vision

1 Leadership, Purpose & Vision: Steps I & II

The Seven Steps

Step 1: Find your Purpose and Catch the Vision
Step 2: Decide to Act and Write the Vision
Step 3: Build a Team to Accomplish the Vision
Step 4: Manage the Team & Foster Innovation
Step 5: Believe in the Vision
Step 6: Run with the Vision
Step 7: Hang on to the Vision

"Leadership is the capacity to translate vision into reality."
--Warren Bennis

"What would you do if you knew you could not fail?" One of Christ's followers said, "…be even more diligent to make your call and election sure, for if you do these things you will never stumble."[1] If you know your calling and do accordingly, you will not stumble. You can do what you are called to do and not even get paid for it, but you can still enjoy it because you find it extremely satisfying and pleasurable. It is like a school of fish swimming in the water or a flock of birds flying in the air; they are created for that purpose and are most comfortable executing on it. Similarly, each one of us has a purpose and once we find it, we are able to execute on it with ease and pleasure. However true these thoughts may be, many do not even attempt to act on their purpose for the fear of failure. But your ancient friend (quoted above) reminds you that if you make your call and election sure, you will not stumble or fail.

The Apostle Paul put it quite appropriately, "Not that I am already attained or am I already perfected; but I press on, that I may lay hold of that for which Christ Jesus has also laid hold of me."[2] Paul understood clearly the concept of God-given purpose. He points out that he is not perfect but presses on to accomplish his purpose. Though God has made you for a purpose, that does not mean that it will be easy. There is an element of pressing on to accomplish your purpose. You need to persevere and act on your purpose to accomplish it. Our Creator reminds us that He has a special plan in mind for each of us: "Your eyes saw my substance, being yet unformed. And in Your book they all were written, the days fashioned for me, when as yet

---

1. *The Holy Bible: New King James Version.* (Nashville, TN: Thomas Nelson, Inc., 1982), 2 Peter 1:10.
2. Philippians 3:12

there were none of them."[3] God has planned each day in your life; He has a plan and purpose for each one of you.

As God has created you, He is the one who knows your purpose. It is therefore God who you should ask for your purpose in life. To fulfill this purpose, God will give you a vision. Not everyone is called to start a ministry, a church or a business. But each one is definitely called to fulfill his or her purpose. You could even be called upon to be part of another person's vision.

Vision is to see something that is far off but coming into view. The Greek word for vision is *hazon*, which means, "to see." The Hebrew word *optasia* means "coming into view." Vision is for a particular purpose, which is not yet a reality but will become a reality if the visionary is willing to pay the price.

Indulge me for a moment as I go back into memory lane when I first began to seriously consider my God-given purpose. I had been working as a chip designer in Silicon Valley and was eventually promoted to Product Marketing Manager. This position took me to 13 countries in less than 18 months, where I was able to launch two products in two continents. During my entire tenure in the corporate world, I knew that I would some day be launching out on my own. In fact, if the truth be told, I can remember having this deep desire early in my high school days. After seven years of valuable experience, I knew the time had arrived for me to act upon this aspiration. In August of 2000, Mindbrook Inc. (www.mindbrook.com) was founded to provide leading edge software for corporate

---

3. Psalm 139:16

management and compliance. The lessons to be learned in the pages of this book can be traced directly to the knowledge gained at Mindbrook.

> "If the vision can be accomplished with your paycheck it is not a God-given vision."
> -- Myles Munroe

Once you discover your God-given purpose and the vision to accomplish that purpose, the next logical step is to take action. You need to resolve for yourself that your vision needs to be accomplished. Most of us do not discover our purpose in life and only a few of us act upon it. There will be questions like: How will I live? How will I support my family? Such questions might convince you to procrastinate or even abandon the decision to act on your vision. Yet, you must understand that God will make a way where there seems to be no way. If you do not take action you will not fulfill your purpose. Myles Munroe, author of the best-selling book, 'The Principles and Power of Vision', says that the graveyard is the most expensive real estate in the world because many hopes and dreams have died there. You should not make the graveyard richer. You must choose to act on your vision.

Once you decide to act on your vision, it is imperative that the vision be written down. God once spoke to Habakkuk, a religious leader in Israel's past, "Write the vision and make it plain on tablets, that he may run who reads it."[4] Habakkuk was troubled by the prosperity and

---

4. Habakkkuk 2:2

Chapter 1: Leadership, Purpose & Vision: Steps I & II

rise to power of the wicked Babylonians both in Judah and its neighbors, Assyria and Egypt. God spoke to him and asked him to write the vision on tablets so that the people could run with it and the tablets containing the vision were in fact not very big. God not only says you need to have a vision, but that it should be succinct and to the point. The reasoning behind writing the vision down is not just so you, yourself can see clearly what lies ahead, but also to allow you to refine it and make it as succinct as possible. Once you write the vision down, it can then be used to share with others in your sphere of influence so that everyone understands the destination and the direction of the vision, allowing those who choose, to follow you. God gives the vision to one person who in turn decides to act on it and share it with others. This will help each person to run with the vision based on his or her part in it.

Leading the Vision

There are many definitions of leadership. Webster's dictionary defines leadership as "the office or position of leading, or capacity to lead, or the act or instance of leading." There are many people in positions of leadership who do not function as leaders. Conversely, you do not need a position or a title to function as a leader.

According to John Maxwell, author of the best-selling book *'Developing the Leader Within You'*, "Leadership is influence".[5] This definition of leadership captures the impact leadership has in influencing others. Fred Smith, founder of FedEx, defines leadership as "getting people to work for you when they are not obligated to."[6] This definition is not my favorite as it focuses on

5. *'Developing the Leader Within You'* by John Maxwell (Nashville, Tennessee by Thomas Nelson Inc. 1993) page 1

obtaining followers. Though it's true that the leader will attract followers because of who he is, leadership should not be defined around that aspect.

Myles Munroe's definition of leadership is defined simply, yet profoundly, as self-discovery. Myles has captured the basic element needed for leadership, which is; understand who you are.

In combining the thoughts of Myles Munroe and John Maxwell with my own, we can create a complete definition of leadership: Leadership is first discovering yourself and your purpose, then influencing and inspiring others to join hands with you to turn that *vision into reality.*

> *Leadership is first discovering yourself and your purpose, then influencing and inspiring others to join hands with you to turn that vision into reality.*

Before you can influence others, you need to discover what your purpose is. William Shakespeare once said, "We know what we are, but know not what we may be." Once you know your life purpose, you 1) know what you may be, 2) become passionate about your purpose, and 3) are able to influence and inspire others to join the voyage.

---

6. heartquotes.net, http://www.heartquotes.net/Leadership.html

Chapter 1: Leadership, Purpose & Vision: Steps I & II

General vs. Unique Purpose

The general purpose your Creator intended for you is to praise and honor His Name. The Lord God says, "This people I have formed for Myself; They shall declare My praise".[7] But there is also a specific and unique purpose for each human being who is born on this earth. Jesus had a specific purpose for his life. His disciples were simple people, fishermen and tax collectors; they were not men of vaunted nobility. Yet Jesus knew His purpose, which in turn influenced His disciples to join hands with Him to fulfill this purpose. Jesus truly is the greatest leader and a model for leadership. In fact, we'll be using his leadership style and stories as examples throughout this book. Jesus has impacted and influenced billions of people around the world. As He continues to influence billions today, He is an undeniably good choice as a model leader.

Your Unique Purpose

Everyone has leadership opportunities. Sociologists tell us that even the most introverted individuals will influence ten thousand other people during his or her lifetime.[8] That means that all of you are leading in some areas, while following in others.

In the creation account God said "Let Us make man in our image, according to Our likeness; let them have dominion over the fish of the sea, over the birds of the air, over the cattle, over all the earth and over every creeping thing that creeps on the earth." God created man to have dominion on the earth.[9] Leadership does not mean that you are the boss, but it means that you have the

---

7. Isaiah 43:2
8. *'Developing the Leader Within You'* by John Maxwell (Nashville, Tennessee by Thomas Nelson Inc. 1993) page 2
9. Genesis 1:26

responsibility to use the talents and skill set with which you have been blessed. Leadership is needed to have order in whatever you do, whether it be at a company, a church, in the family, at school, or wherever people are gathered together in order to achieve something.

> **"What you don't do can be a destructive force."**
> **-- Eleanor Roosevelt**

"All excellence involves discipline and tenacity of purpose," says John W. Gardner, former secretary of the US Department of Health, Education and Welfare.[10] Recognizing your God-given purpose in life will propel you and motivate you to run the race to accomplish this purpose.

> **As God has created us, He is the one who knows this path and our true purpose.**

You can't expect to accomplish your purpose or have others join you if you don't know the specific path you are meant to take. As God has created you, He is the one who knows this path and your true purpose. Each of you, therefore, should ask God for your unique purpose in life. Finding your unique purpose is vitally important to building a team to accomplish your purpose.

---

10. *'Excellence: Can We Be Equal and Excellent Too'* John W Gardner (W.W. Norton & Company,1995),76.

Leadership, Purpose and Vision

**Summary
Principles**

Leadership is first discovering yourself and your purpose, then influencing and inspiring others to join hands with you to turn the _____ into _____. Leadership does not mean that you are the _____, but it means that you have the _____. To fulfill this purpose God will give you a _____.

Seven steps necessary to move from vision to reality

01) _____

02) _____

03) _____

04) _____

05) _____

06) _____

07) _____

**Life
Application**

1. In which areas are you a leader and in which areas are you a follower?

2. What is the God-given purpose for your life? (If you are still seeking God to identify the God-given purpose, say so!)

3. What is the vision that will accomplish this purpose? Write the vision clearly. (Keep it succinct, you should be able to write it on paper. Take your time. As George Bernard Shaw said, "I wrote you a long letter as I did not have time to write a short one.")

2 Team Building: Step III

The Seven Steps

Step 1: Find your Purpose and Catch the Vision
Step 2: Decide to Act and Write the Vision
Step 3: Build a Team to Accomplish the Vision
Step 4: Manage the Team & Foster Innovation
Step 5: Believe in the Vision
Step 6: Run with the Vision
Step 7: Hang on to the Vision

*"Leaders do not force people to follow them –
they invite them on a journey."*
-- Charles S. Lauer

"It takes teamwork to make your dream work."
-- John Maxwell

Throughout history, nothing of significance has ever been accomplished by a lone individual. You can look at the last 5,000 years and think about the leaders who've emerged and focused on achieving specific objectives (good or bad) and one common thing you will notice is each of them had a team around them. John Craig has said, "No matter how much work a man can do, no matter how engaging his personality may be, he will not advance far in business if he cannot work through others."[11] Alexander Graham Bell said, "Great discoveries and improvements invariably involve the cooperation of many minds."[12]

> **"If you are a leader and there is no one following you, you are just taking a walk."**
> **-- Chinese Proverb**

Where there is no vision, people have nothing to follow. But one also needs to understand that without people, the vision will never come to pass. So it is very important to build a strong team to execute the vision. You become a leader when you know your purpose and persevere through all circumstances to accomplish it. Seeing your determination, others will join hands with you and recognize you as a leader.

---

11. 'Reinvent Yourself' by Hal Gieseking (Business Scribe Inc.), 127 http://tinyurl.com/2hl95u
12. dailycelebrations.com, http://www.dailycelebrations.com/discovery.htm

In building a team, you also need to think about the size and scope of your vision. If the vision is one of Mount Everest sized proportions, then a team capable of scaling Everest will be needed.

The quality of the team you need is based upon the scope of the vision.

Steps for Team Building

Step 1. Ask for and seek guidance. Throughout history great leaders sought divine guidance from the Creator as well as seeking counsel from their mentors and advisors. For example, Jesus himself fasted and prayed for forty days and forty nights before he began his ministry and started recruiting his team.

Step 2. Explain the vision clearly and what problems it solves. You should not share the vision with everyone, as there will be people who will discourage you and will not be able to understand the vision. The leader needs to have a clear understanding of the team structure and what skill-sets will be needed on the core team. People with appropriate skills or gifts need to be identified so that they are able to accomplish the vision. As you meet people and build relationships, choose the prospects of your team and then share the vision with them either one on one or in a vision casting session. As you are casting a vision, you should inspire the team by painting a picture of the future and how it will look. Your commitment and passion for the vision can be demonstrated with stories that explain how you have come to this point and the price that was paid to get there.

> *Use the word "we" rather than "I"*

Step 3. Explain where you will get the resources you need. The team members will want to know how the necessary resources will be obtained. In ancient Jerusalem, Nehemiah cast a vision to rebuild the city's walls. He told the team about God's favor and the King's willingness to provide the resources to accomplish the vision. God provided through the king the finances and authority Nehemiah needed to accomplish the vision.[13]

Step 4. Get a positive response from the team before assigning them a role on it. In our example above, Nehemiah waited for feedback and a positive response from the people to kick-off the project. When the people said, "Let us rise up and build," the project started.[14] The team members will complement each other and the leader assigns specific roles to each team member based on their gifts. This will eliminate the impact of their weaknesses. Peter Drucker, the Father of management science is a proponent of this concept.

---

13. Nehemiah 2:17
14. Nehemiah 2:18

> *"Creation is the victory of persuasion and not of force."*
> *-- Ancient Greek Philosopher*

Step 5. Continue to build and motivate a committed team. Inspire the team members to do better things than they are currently doing. When Jesus said, "Follow me and I will make you fishers of men,"[15] He was conveying the idea that these simple fishermen will no longer be just catching fish but will be influencing and transforming the communities around them.

Qualities you Need to Look for in Team Members

1. **Select ones who are willing to pay the price for the vision.** The ones who are willing to sacrifice are those who will persevere with the vision. Ones who are not willing to pay the price will walk away from the vision when a storm comes. Select team members who align with the vision, not hirelings or volunteers.

2. **Select ones with integrity.** It is a good idea to check references. Moreover he must have a good testimony among those who are outside.[16] You need people on your team whose references recommend them with enthusiasm and confidence.

3. **Select ones with leadership potential.** If everyone is proactive and takes leadership roles in their specific assignments, then the team will work well. Jesus chose Matthew,

---

15. Matthew 4:19
16. 1 Timothy 3:7

who was a tax collector, to be on his team. As a tax collector, Matthew was in a position of authority and leadership interacting with people.[17]

4. **Select ones with wisdom, intelligence, knowledge and one who is quick to learn.** Behind every great leader you find men and women "gifted in all wisdom, possessing knowledge and quick to understand".[18]

5. **Select ones who are hardworking.** Jesus chose fishermen on his team –who have to rise up early in the morning and work very hard.[19] There is no substitute for hard work.

Motivating the Team

During my current associate professorship at Bethany University, I had an opportunity to advise students on their research projects. There was an interesting project that one of my students had undertaken to improve the morale at the pharmacy where she worked. She did a survey called the "Major Dreams" survey to find out what are the key morale issues at the pharmacy. The four most important items on the list were communication, celebration, teamwork and accountability. There were four hypotheses, which were evaluated for improving morale.

1. Regular team meetings with participative leadership style to solve problems will increase respect and trust among employees.

2. By celebrating, we will increase communication and laughter among employees.

---

17. Matthew 9:9
18. Daniel 1:4
19. Matthew 4:18-19

3. Customer service classes will improve listening skills not only for the customers benefit, but internally as well.

4. By redefining job tasks, productivity and morale will increase.

The four hypotheses were evaluated with specific points to gauge effectiveness with the following results. Three out of the four hypotheses were found to be true. Customer service training had the most effect on morale. Empowering employees with necessary customer service skills lifted their spirits and gave them the knowledge and tools for greater patient care. Celebrations had the second greatest effect on morale. Celebrations opened up conversations between employees. They laughed more and were beginning to actually like each other. Also, as the leader acknowledged his team members whenever he got a chance rather than just once a month, employees' spirits were raised even higher. Team building activities had the third highest impact on morale. The team members began to feel safe voicing their opinions. They felt that what they had to say mattered and there would be no repercussions. Finally, task assignments did not have any impact on the morale.

All leaders need to develop and train team members. Leaders need to be evaluating where the team members are and where it is they need to go to in order to most effectively plan the training sessions. Not only should the leader be continually learning; he also should encourage the team members to learn and improve as well. The people on the team are the key value proposition for any organization. It is interesting that just having celebrations like potlucks improved the communication and laughter among employees thus improving morale. As a leader, you need to provide an environment of trust and also give an opportunity to build relationships among the team members. Not only should you build a team and have strong personal relationships, you should also help the team members build strong relationships among themselves.

Jethro, Moses' father-in-law saw that Moses alone was judging the people from morning to evening. He suggested to Moses to form team leaders to judge people, as Moses cannot handle all the cases by himself. The team leaders based on their capabilities can handle a plethora of people. Only in situations that cannot be resolved by them would Moses become involved. Moses listened to the wise counsel of his father-in-law and formed a team to efficiently judge the people.[20]

You need to learn to work through others by developing leaders around you. Determine yourself to build the appropriate team to accomplish and multiply the vision.

---

20. Exodus 18:13-26

Team Building

**Summary
Principles**

Steps for Team Building

01)_____

02)_____

03)_____

04)_____

05)_____

Qualities you need to look for in team members

01)_____

02)_____

03)_____

04)_____

05)_____

**Life
Application**

1. Do you pray for your team regularly?

2. Do you use the word 'We' rather than 'I'?

3. Do you have a checklist before you recruit a team member? If not, what will be your checklist? If yes, what is your current checklist?

3 Leadership Qualities: Step IV, Part I

The Seven Steps

Step 1: Find your Purpose and Catch the Vision
Step 2: Decide to Act and Write the Vision
Step 3: Build a Team to Accomplish the Vision
Step 4: Manage the Team & Foster Innovation
Step 5: Believe in the Vision
Step 6: Run with the Vision
Step 7: Hang on to the Vision

"The first step to leadership is servanthood."
--John Maxwell

"Management is efficiency in climbing the ladder; leadership determines whether the ladder is leaning against the right wall."
-- Stephen Covey

Winston Churchill is best remembered as a statesman, politician and world leader who saved the world from Nazi domination in the dark days of the Second World War. On May 10, 1940, Winston Churchill became Prime Minister of England. When he met with his Cabinet on May 13, he told them that "I have nothing to offer but blood, toil, tears and sweat."[21] It was clear from this story that this great historical leader understood some of the key qualities of a leader: perseverance, compassion and sacrifice.

> *"Genius is one percent inspiration and ninety nine percent perspiration."*
> *--Thomas Edison*

Leaders are Hardworking

Leaders must be hard workers, typically they are the ones who should be first to arrive and last to leave. Churchill was known to work tirelessly each day into the wee hours of the morning, stopping only to take a ninety-minute mid-day nap. Many of the world's famous inventors would go days without food or sleep in the midst of their greatest breakthrough. Modeling this ethic of hard work and sacrifice will instill the values necessary in your team to persevere to accomplish the vision.

---

21. The Churchill Centre, Washington, D.C., http://www.winstonchurchill.org

> *"I want to be thoroughly used up when I die, for the harder I work, the more I live. Life is a sort of splendid torch, which I hold for a moment. And I want to make it burn brightly, before I hand it off to future generations."*
> *-- George Bernard Shaw*

Leaders are Able to Face Challenges Alone

Leaders need to be willing to run the race alone. At times, leaders must be like eagles that fly alone. Mohandas K. Gandhi, father of modern India, wrote to the President of the Indian National Congress in 1942 to resign as their leader. Gandhiji said in the letter it was his belief that only nonviolence can save India and the world from self-extinction. He went on to state that he must continue his mission whether he is alone or assisted by an organization or individuals. Gandhiji was focused on his mission of independence for India through non-violence and he was willing to work alone towards achieving his vision.

> *If you are willing to run alone, many will follow you.*

Leaders are Loving and Compassionate

Leaders should have a passion and love for the vision as well as love for the team sharing the vision.

> *God sent a leader, Jesus Christ, to save the world and He loved us so much that He died for us so that we can have eternal life.*

One of the greatest examples of leadership is the prophet Moses. His vision from God was to lead the Israelites from Egypt into the Promised Land. While Moses was on Mount Sinai receiving the Ten Commandments, the Israelites lost patience and began to worship idols rather than give honor to the true God. God was ready to destroy the whole nation because of their sin. Moses as a leader had great love for his people. He pleaded to God for mercy and God spared those that were willing to turn back to him.

> *"Leadership is all about love."*
> *-- Tom Peters*

Another leader in history who was motivated by compassion was Abraham Lincoln. He often attended private funerals out of sheer compassion, which in turn inspired trust, loyalty and admiration from soldiers and subordinates alike. At one point in his career, he worked for a top lawyer named Edwin Stanton. He sat and learned from him but was hurt by his daily contempt and hubris. He had to make a conscious decision to forgive the hurt and even went so far as to choose Stanton as a member of his cabinet.[22] Although this idea of forgiveness is rarely addressed when discussing team dynamics, the absence of offenses between members of the team will go a long way in creating the type of synergy necessary for success.

Leaders are People of Ethics and Integrity

Leaders must be ethical and people of integrity. If you have committed to do a particular thing then you must follow through even if you find out later that it will hurt you.[23]

David Packard (one of the founders of Hewlett Packard) dropped out from his CEO club, as he was not comfortable discussing ways to squeeze more profit from the business. He believed, "A company has greater responsibility than making money for its stockholders."[24] His strong values disseminated throughout the organization and no doubt significantly factored in the company's success.

In the early 80's, Johnson & Johnson faced a crisis when cyanide was found in their Tylenol product, eventually leading to a recall which cost the company $100,000,000. Within hours of the discovery, the company made the decision to recall knowing full well the financial ramifications. Later the CEO explained that it was an easy decision based on their credo. They stuck with their credo exhibiting high integrity despite the cost.

---

22. 'Abraham Lincoln' by Thomas Keneally (Penguin Lives, Viking Adult, Dec. 2002), 59
23. Psalm 15
24. The Ten Greatest CEO's of all Time by Jim Collins (Fortune Magazine July 21 2003), 56

Leaders are Honest

Webster's dictionary defines honesty as "fairness and straightforwardness of conduct or sincerity or uprightness of character or action." Honesty implies the refusal to lie, steal or deceive in any way. You expect your leader to be honest. Honesty builds trust among your team. This is one key in gaining respect and commitment.

Leaders are Forward-Looking

> "The longer you look back the farther you can look forward."
> -- Winston Churchill

Being forward-looking means the leader has to be a visionary who is able to envision the future. You need to learn from your personal past and from history so you can see much further. This ties in directly to our earlier discussion about finding your purpose and vision from God. Though the Lord has called all of us with a purpose, there are only a few people who understand their purpose and have a vision for their life. While talking to a young woman, about 24-years of age, I posed to her a question: "What is the purpose of your life?" Her simple response was a typical "I don't know." Sadly, a lot of us do not know our purpose nor do we have a vision for our lives.

As leaders, when you are forward-looking and able to cast a vision, then you will find many willing to follow you. Only a leader who is forward-looking will know the way and be able to lead his team in that direction. He needs to press towards accomplishing the vision. Apostle Paul says, "I press toward the goal for the prize of the upward call of God in Christ Jesus."[25] He was a forward-looking man and he clearly understood his goal and vision for his life

Leaders are Inspiring

> *"Inspired people inspire people."*
> *-- Myles Munroe*

An effective leader has to have an enlivening and exalting influence on the team creating a passion for the cause among them. And as Jesus walked by the Sea of Galilee, He saw Simon and Andrew his brother casting a net into the sea; for they were fishermen. Then Jesus said to them, "Follow Me, and I will make you become fishers of men."[26] They immediately left their nets and followed Him. Jesus gave his disciples an inspiration to do better things than what they were currently doing. At that point, they were but fishermen, but now they had a greater opportunity to influence others, to follow Jesus, and fulfill their vision.

Leaders are Competent

> *"Belief + talent + experience + wisdom = competence"*
> *-- Frank Mitchell*

One thing you must believe and accept is that you have been given the talents and abilities needed to accomplish your vision. In addition,

---

25. Philippians 3:14
26. Matthew 4:19

you need to have the requisite experience, education and skills to lead. As my friend Frank and I were reviewing this concept (he happens to be the editor of this book), he commented that all of these qualities mentioned above would be for naught if the leader didn't possess the wisdom and knowledge necessary to apply them.

Leaders are Credible

The dictionary defines "credible" as "offering reasonable grounds for being believed." A combination of integrity, honesty and competence makes the leader credible.

Franklin Roosevelt, in one of his famous fireside chats on the economy in April of 1938, acknowledged, "I never forget that I live in a house owned by all the American people and that I have been given their trust."

Leaders are Courageous

> "The only thing we have to fear is fear itself."
> -- Franklin Roosevelt

Courage gives confidence and must be based on conviction. What does courage mean? It is to step out in faith and take risks. It is to exercise discernment with confidence, boldness and willingness to face resistance. Katherine Graham took over the "Washington Post" as an accidental CEO when her husband died and she turned a regional newspaper into a major national publication through her willingness to cover the Watergate scandal. Graham's newspaper covered this story despite constant threat and pressure from the Nixon led White House. Graham never flinched remaining bold and courageous; a testament to her strength of vision.

Leaders are Able to Preempt Problems

Leaders will not wait until a problem or a challenge has been created. They will preempt problems and hence be able prevent crisis. This quality is clearly a complement of being forward-thinking.

Leaders are Able to Grow and Develop Continuously

> *"To teach is to learn twice."*
> *-- Joseph Joubert*

Leaders are lifelong learners. One needs to read, study and take or teach courses in order to continually grow and develop. Seek out the advice of others by establishing mentoring relationships. If you have a problem, you should not ask a peer for advice, but someone who is more experienced. A case in point is Sam Walton, founder of Wal-Mart. He was known for his hunger for learning and traveled extensively worldwide to understand the key to successful retail business. Wal-Mart now is one of the largest companies in the whole world.

Leaders are Able to See the Big Picture

Boeing built bombers and planes that helped to win World War II, but once the war was over, its revenues plummeted 90%. Everyone else thought of Boeing as a company that simply built bombers. Boeing's head, Bill Allen, saw it as a company, which built flying machines. Had he stuck with the original vision and not seen the larger picture, the company would not have survived. This allowed Boeing to move into the commercial market allowing it to become one of the leading manufacturers of airplanes to this day.

A Long List Although the qualities of being an effective leader are long and strenuous, looking at it should not be overwhelming. In considering the qualities above, you must first understand your personal strengths and weaknesses. You should focus on your strengths and bring in team members who can make-up for your weaknesses, thus creating a complementary team that can accomplish the vision.

Leadership Qualities

Summary Principles

The Leadership qualities listed in this chapter. Leaders are:

01) _____

02) _____

03) _____

04) _____

05) _____

06) _____

07) _____

08) _____

09) _____

10) _____

11) _____

12) _____

13) _____

Life Application

1. What are the top 5 leadership qualities (You can add qualities not mentioned in the chapter)?

2. Which leadership qualities do you possess (Please list them)?

3. Which leadership qualities do you want to develop (Please list them)?

4. Which leadership qualities do you recognize a need to develop (Please list them)?

5. How can you begin to develop these leadership qualities?

4 Leadership and Management: Step IV, Part II

The Seven Steps

Step 1: Find your Purpose and Catch the Vision
Step 2: Decide to Act and Write the Vision
Step 3: Build a Team to Accomplish the Vision
Step 4: Manage the Team & Foster Innovation
Step 5: Believe in the Vision
Step 6: Run with the Vision
Step 7: Hang on to the Vision

A key fact that one must understand is that management and leadership are not the same thing. With this in mind, let's explore these terms further.

According to most management texts, there are four basic functions of management: planning, organizing, leading and controlling. The classic view has left out vision as one of the basic functions of management. Without a clear vision utilizing these basic functions of management will not ensure success. A leader needs to be able to both state the vision and be able to manage it; i.e. plan, organize, lead, control.

The vision will be a guide to the entire organization and the team to decide what to do and what not to do. It will be a compass for the company, guiding them as they challenge themselves to go from *vision to reality*.

Planning is a process that managers use to identify and select appropriate goals and courses of action. Organizing is a process that managers use to establish a structure of working relationships that allow the organizational members to interact and cooperate to achieve organizational goals. In leading, managers not only articulate a clear vision for organizational members to follow but also energize and enable members to understand the part they play in achieving stated goals. This is how management textbooks define leading as one component of management. Leading is needed in every component of management and vision is important enough to be included as a core function of it. "In controlling, managers evaluate how well an organization is achieving its goals and take action to maintain or improve performance."[27]

_____

27. '*Contemporary Management*' by Gareth R. Jones and Jennifer M. George, 3rd ed. (New York: McGraw-Hill, 2003), 11

Planning

Vision

Leading

Organizing

Controlling

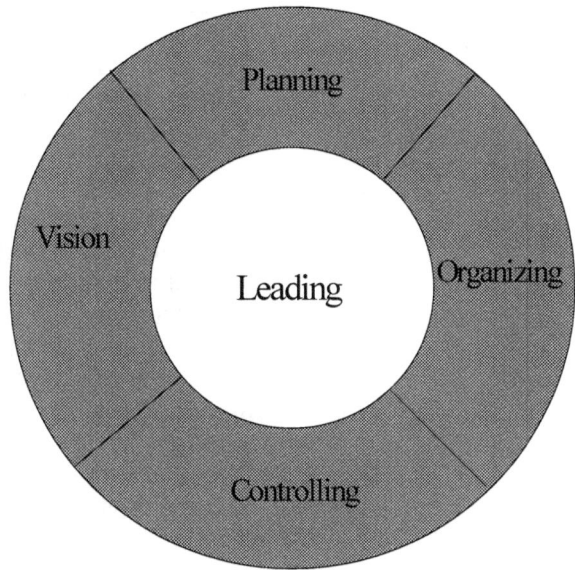

The key point about the basic functions of management is that they are not independent functions connected to each other in sequence as is shown in most management text books. Leadership is actually at the heart of planning, organizing, control and vision. As John Maxwell says, "Everything rises and falls on leadership."[28] Leading is a function, which impacts each of the other functions of management and can be illustrated with the hub-and-spoke model shown above.

---

28. *'Developing the Leader Within You'* by John Maxwell (Nashville, Tennessee by Thomas Nelson Inc. 1993), Introduction

> *"I will pay more for the ability to deal with people than any other ability under the sun."*
> *--John D. Rockefeller*

Let's address the importance of planning and not get into the organizing and controling aspect of management in this book. A "plan" is defined in Webster's dictionary as "a method for achieving an end or an orderly arrangement of parts of an overall design or objective." **This means that to accomplish a vision, you need to have a methodology or a plan.** There are many choices for you to make in your life and there are various opportunities you can explore. They might sound like good plans, but you need to adopt God's plan for your life based on your individual purpose and vision. God has planned each day of your life; The Apostle Paul instructs us; "Just as He chose us in Him before the foundation of the world...having predestined us to adoption as sons by Jesus Christ to Himself..."[29] God has predestined you as His children and chose you even before the foundation of the world. He knew you even before He created the earth. Your responsibility is to find out God's purpose for your life and fulfill it. God will give you a vision to fulfill the purpose in your life.

---

29. Ephesians 1:4-5

> *"An average person with average talents and average education can outstrip genius if they have clear focused goals."*
> *-- Mary Kay*

Aligning to your God-given vision leads you to achieve the full potential He has placed within you. You need to plan to accomplish this vision. Churchill once stated that it is best to, "Ponder and then act." Churchill would do well to add prayer to the mix.

A wise king once said, "A man's heart plans his way, but the Lord directs his steps".[30] If you depend on God and acknowledge Him, he will guide you in every step. As you commit everything to God, the Lord will give you wisdom to develop successful plans.

If you truly want to fulfill your Creator's purpose, leaving Him in your purpose not only makes sense, but leaving him out of it may lead to disaster. Doctor Luke in ancient Israel, talks about a rich man who had a bountiful yield and was planning to build larger barns to store all his crops and goods. He wanted to do this, thinking that he could take it easy and enjoy the rest of his life. God called him a fool and said that he would die the same day and the treasures he had laid up for himself would be of no use.[31]

---

30. Proverbs 16:9
31. Luke 12:16-20

Step 1. Understand God's purpose & vision for your life. How do you understand God's purpose in your life? You may have been carrying a particular desire or dream in your heart, which may have been birthed in childhood. It may return later in your youth or early adulthood. It seems to just keep following you and coming back to your heart and mind. This is one-way God can talk to you and begin to form His purpose in your life. In addition to this significant way of speaking to us, God will also use scripture and the counsel of others, as well as dreams and visions.

Step 2. Align yourself to God's purpose and set long and short-term goals for each role you play. All of you play different roles as pastor, sister, brother, spouse, volunteer, employee, parent, etc. You need to set goals for each role you play. Write the goals down. You spend a lot of time making grocery lists, but little time writing down goals that can affect the course of your life.

Step 3. Align yourself with the goals and plan your weeks and months. The gospel talks about how someone who intends to build a tower sits down first and calculates the cost and plans the activity.

Step 4. Be wise, align yourself with the weekly plans and plan your time accordingly. Time management is key to becoming a successful leader. You should choose your activities according to your purpose and goals. It might be a "good thing," but it might not be the right thing to do. You sometimes waste a lot of time hanging out with friends and having a barbeque or watching TV. Everyone has twenty-four hours a day; those who manage their time with wisdom will be more effective. Sometimes participating in a particular project like teaching Sunday school or attending a conference might not be the right thing to do if it is not going to help you accomplish your purpose.

More than Fifty years ago Sir Edmund Hillary and Tenzing Norgay conquered Mount Everest. Eric Shipton was the key member in four of England's seven expeditions to Everest. So he was chosen by the Himalayan Committee to lead the 1953 attempt to conquer Everest. Eric Shipton was a very talented climber and his improvisational climbs had shown entrepreneurial flair. But his inattention to detail and planning were notorious. On one trip he even forgot his backpack. The Committee fired Eric Shipton within six weeks of choosing him to lead. The Committee was not replacing a person but replacing an old idea with a new one: the challenge was too big to depend on one man's talent and character, instead needing what some call the "art of organization." Col. John Hunt was the person driving this strategy and was the very picture of a modern professional manager. He even specified that each box of ration contain 29 tins of sardines. His strategy, which soon became a standard in mountaineering, called for an army of climbers, sherpas, porters and yaks that would methodically move up the mountain, shuttling supplies to ever-higher camps. Hunt said the desire to reach the top should be both individual and collective.[32] Through Hunt's achievements you can now begin to understand the importance of planning and teamwork.

How to Stick to the Plan

1. **Always depend on God**. In an ancient book of wisdom it states, "Trust in the Lord with all your heart, and lean not on your own understanding."[33]

2. **Lead a disciplined sacrificial life.** Leadership starts with leading yourself first before you can lead others. Personal discipline is critical to sticking to the plan. Jesus once said to those aspiring to leadership in His "start-up" church, "If anyone desires to come after Me, let him deny himself, and take up his cross daily and follow Me."[34] It's not about what you want to do. There is an element of personal sacrifice you must continually embrace in accomplishing your God given purpose. In this you will achieve success and significance that nothing else in your life can equal.

3. **Set your priorities right**. Lacking the skill to set the right priorities will hinder your ability to stick to the plan. Wasting resources on low priority actions is a sure way to stifle the execution of the plan. You must agree with your team ahead of time on what priorities will accelerate the execution of the plan with the resources available.

---

32. *The Board that Conquered Everest*, (Fortune, Oct 27, 2003)
33. Proverbs 3:5
34. Luke 9:23

A man approached JP Morgan, held up an envelope and said, "Sir, in my hand I hold a guaranteed formula for success, which I will gladly sell you for $25,000." "Sir", JP Morgan replied, "I do not know what is in the envelope, however if you show me, and I like it, I give you my word as a gentleman that I will pay you what you ask." The man agreed to the terms and handed over the envelope. JP Morgan opened it and extracted a single sheet of paper. He gave it one look, a mere glance, and then handed the piece of paper back to the gent. And paid him the agreed upon $25,000. The paper read:

1. Every morning, write a list of things that need to be done that day.
2. Do them.[35]

---

35. "TP's 'Top 41' Quotes," Tom Peters Co., http://www.tom-peters.com/blogs/main/PDFs/Quotes41_010306_3.pdf

Leadership and Management

The five basic functions of management are:

01)_____

02)_____

03)_____

04)_____

05)_____

Steps to Effective Planning for Your Life

01)_____

02)_____

03)_____

04)_____

How to stick to the Plan

01)_____

02)_____

03)_____

1. What are the roles you play (e.g., CEO, Pastor, spouse, sibling, employee, board member, etc.)?

2. What are your long-term goals for your top two roles (Extend later to all your roles)?

3. What are your short-term goals for your top two roles (Extend later to all your roles)?

4. Write down your weekly and daily plan (Focus on activities you will repeat, e.g., team meeting, sales meeting, etc.).

5 Foster Innovation: Step IV, Part III

The Seven Steps

Step 1: Find your Purpose and Catch the Vision
Step 2: Decide to Act and Write the Vision
Step 3: Build a Team to Accomplish the Vision
Step 4: Manage the Team & Foster Innovation
Step 5: Believe in the Vision
Step 6: Run with the Vision
Step 7: Hang on to the Vision

As you continue to manage your team, you need to foster and promote innovation within the organization. Fostering innovation could be the key difference in helping to out-think and defeat the competition. You need to hear team members' input as to how to improve efficiency while making their jobs less labor intensive. The team understands what they do better than anyone and their recommendations are useful in improving the organization. Sony was one of first companies in Japan who started to get input from team members for ways to improve product quality.

Steps to Foster Innovation

1. **Allow the team members to spend 15-20% of their time on side projects.** 3M was one of the first companies who allowed team members to spend 15% of their time on projects of their choosing. The Post-It product was an innovation, which came from a side project, which still rakes in billions of dollars in revenues for 3M today. Former CEO William McKnight turned innovation into a systematic, repeatable process. He said, "While you could not predict exactly what this system would create, you could predict with certainty that it would create."[36] Eric Schmidt, CEO of Google asserts that, "Everything new here comes out of the time engineers spend on side projects. It certainly does not come from management."[37] Google allows its engineers to spend 20% of their time on side projects.

2. **Encourage the team to challenge the status quo.** Leaders should always question the status quo and challenge it. After his burning bush encounter with God, Moses questioned why the Israelites were in bondage and wanted to challenge and change that situation. Nobody believed the Wright brothers could ever fly; later no one

---

36. *The Ten Greatest CEO's of all Time* By Jim Collins (Fortune Magazine July 21 2003), 58
37. *Titans of Business* with John Battelle (Business 2.0 December 2005), 136

believed that the sound barrier could be broken in an airplane, and, even later, the notion of sending a man to the moon was considered ludicrous.

3. **Build a motivated team**. One way to keep the team motivated is to help them reach apexes they would not be able to go themselves. Jesus gave his disciples a higher calling by making them "fishers of men" rather than common fishermen[38]. Once a team is inspired to reach their full potential that they would be unable to reach on their own, they will gladly join hands with you to work towards your vision. When motivated, team members who are challenged with the vision and given the authority and responsibility, will innovate to overcome any and all challenges.

4. **Train the team and give them a chance to fail**. As leaders, you need to spend time with your team to teach and train, as well as learn, from them. Give people space to operate in. Give them a chance to fail. A CEO of a fortune 100 company once had a senior executive team member make a wrong decision causing several millions of dollars to be lost for the company. The executive was convinced that he would be fired the next day, so when he went to his boss the following day and asked his boss about it. His boss said, "I just invested several million dollars in you, how can I fire you?"

---

38. Matthew 4:19

5. **Say thanks; reward not only accomplishments, but also failures**. You need to acknowledge and encourage team members for their contribution. People are looking for recognition and you need to give it to them at the appropriate time. Abraham Lincoln had a kind word, an encouraging smile and a humorous remark for all people he talked to. He knew that people liked to be complimented.[39]

Make sure you thank your team members and reward their accomplishments. The reward could be a phone call to say thank you or recognition in a group meeting. You should reward the team even if they fail if you know that they had tried their best and attempted to reach some lofty goals, which had never been attempted previously. This will send a signal that failure is not penalized. If failure is penalized, the team will not take enough risk, which can often kill innovation. Of course there are times when failure is due to negligence and/or poor performance. Those failures cannot be accepted and need to be addressed.

6. **Teach the leadership team to take responsibility for failure and give the credit away for success.** If the team knows that their leaders are standing with them and are for them, they will do their best. As leaders, you need to model this principle: if there is a failure, take responsibility for it; if there is success, give the credit away. Many leaders do just the

---

39. '*Lincoln on Leadership*' by Donald T. Phillips, (Warner Books, Inc., 1992),18

opposite: taking responsibility for success and happily passing the buck when things fail.

> *I may be given credit for having blazed the trail but when I look at the subsequent developments, I feel the credit is due to others rather than to myself."*
> *--Alexander Graham Bell*

Foster Innovation

Summary Principles

Steps to foster innovation

01)_____

02)_____

03)_____

04)_____

05)_____

06)_____

Life Application

1. Are you applying the fundamental practices of innovation?

2. Which ones are you applying?

3. Which ones are you not applying?

4. Set yourself goals with a timeline to start applying these principles.

6 Leadership and Faith: Step V

The Seven Steps

| Step 1: Find your Purpose and Catch the Vision |
| Step 2: Decide to Act and Write the Vision |
| Step 3: Build a Team to Accomplish the Vision |
| Step 4: Manage the Team & Foster Innovation |
| **Step 5: Believe in the Vision** |
| Step 6: Run with the Vision |
| Step 7: Hang on to the Vision |

"A leader is a dealer in hope."
-- Napoleon Bonaparte

"You never know how much you really believe anything until its truth or falsehood becomes a matter of life or death to you."
-- C.S. Lewis

There is a somewhat abstract indefinable element necessary in accomplishing one's vision or purpose. Some call it fate, others call it their epiphany and some simplify it down to blind luck. Here we will give the credit to faith. Faith helps you to see the vision accomplished even before you start working towards it. You need to believe in the vision and run with it with faith. Faith is the evidence of things not seen and hence you need to "walk by faith and not by sight."[40] As the vision is not yet accomplished, you cannot physically see it, but you see it through your eyes of faith.

> *"Faith is the substance of things hoped for and evidence of things not seen."*
> *-- Heb 11:1*

US President Roosevelt once said, "The only limit to our realization of tomorrow will be our doubts of today. Let us move forward with strong and active faith."[41] Webster's dictionary says that evidence is an outward sign or something that furnishes proof. Faith furnishes proof for your vision. If you are truly on track with your divinely inspired purpose, the vision will come to pass at the appointed time and you should continue working towards it. Perhaps one of the most outlandish examples of this can be found with, Noah, who was divinely warned of the coming flood and by faith built an ark that would rival the Titanic. In fact, history tells us that Noah's design

---

40. 2 Corinthians 5:7
41. Quotationspage.com, http://www.quotation-spage.com/quote/37962.html

was far superior.[42] I am sure many people called him foolish, but he was walking by faith in the purpose he was given.

> *Noah built a huge boat 600 miles from any source of water and claimed it would rain on the earth when in fact the climate of the day never produced one raindrop.*

As leaders, when God gives you an assignment you should 'just do it,' despite challenges and opposition you might encounter. Henry Ford was a young mechanic working for a company in Michigan. After a long day at work, he came home and worked in a shed at the back of his house, hoping to invent a new kind of engine. Everybody around him thought he was wasting his time and called him a "crackpot." Henry Ford, encouraged by the mutual faith of his wife, continued the work and walked by faith. After three years, the new engine became a reality and the horseless carriage was born and a powerful new industry was created.[43]

Another excellent example of someone who walked by faith is George Muller. When God put it into the heart of George Muller to build orphanages in Bristol, England, he had only two shillings (50 cents) in his pocket. Without making his wants known to any man, but to God alone, over a million four hundred thousand pounds ($7,000,000) was sent to him for the building and

---

42. Heb 11:7
43. *'How to Help Your Husband Get Ahead'* by Mrs. Dale Carnegie (Greystone Press 1965)

maintaining of those orphan homes. In all the years since the first orphans arrived, God provided through various means enough food day by day so that they never missed a meal.[44]

What are you Saying? The very world, in which we now live, according to the ancient writings of Moses, was created by the power of our Creator's spoken word. When the Almighty saw the current status of the earth that was without form and dark, He said, "Let there be light" and there was light. Throughout each event of creation God spoke the world into existence. God has created man in His own image so what you say can also have creative power.[45]

> "Let all the earth fear the LORD; Let all the inhabitants of the world stand in awe of Him. For He spoke and it was done."
> -- Psalms 33:9

You can speak positive or negative things for your life and you may have a direct impact on what happens to you. How many people have you met who are negative and speak negative words and are very successful? I have yet to meet one. Death and life are in the power of the tongue and those who love it will eat its fruit.[46] This means that you can speak positive things

---

44. Christian Biography Resources: George Muller, Wholesome Words, http://www.wholesome-words.org/biography/bmuller2.html.
45. Genesis 1:1-26
46. Proverbs 18:21

and maintain a positive attitude and win. The opposite is also true that you can speak negative things and maintain a bad attitude and lose. Typically you think in your heart and then speak the words. Your thoughts are related to your words and can hold the power to bring success or failure.

When Jesus was training his disciples to work for change in the community he asserted, "For assuredly, I say to you, whoever says to this mountain, 'Be removed and be cast into the sea,' and does not doubt in his heart, but believes that those things he says will be done, he will have whatever he says."[47] When leaders face a mountain in front of them, what do they do? As a leader, you will face a lot of mountains as you move towards executing your vision. You need to maintain a positive attitude and continue to work towards overcoming that mountain without doubting. Keep speaking words of encouragement and victory to the team members working with you and success will eventually be yours.

> *"Before you can inspire with emotion, you must be swamped with it yourself. Before you can move their tears, your own must flow. To convince them you must yourself believe."*
> *-- Winston Churchill*

Did you hear the story about a failed Mount Everest expedition? The leader of the expedition called for a dinner before the team went back home. It was a very somber evening and as the

---

47. Mark 11:23

dinner progressed the leader of the expedition came to greet the team members. He turned around and looked at the wall-sized picture of Mount Everest and spoke with resolve and conviction, "You have defeated us in this attempt to conquer you, Mount Everest. You are as big as you can get but we can get better. We will conquer you next year." The team did return and conquered Mount Everest the following year.

As much as the positive words are key for positive results, negative words often lead to negative results. In the Bible, prior to the birth of Christ we read that Zacharias did not believe the angel of the Lord when he appeared to him and told him that his wife Elizabeth would bear a son. He did not believe as he and Elizabeth were well advanced in years. The angel said Zacharias would become mute until their son was born. God wanted to make sure that he does not speak negative words to spoil God's plan.

Your passion in communicating with your team and encouraging them, will fuel action. You will see what you have been saying come to pass.

You should have the faith to run the race with total confidence and as you run, you should keep speaking positively.

Leadership and Faith

Summary Principles

You should walk by _____ and not by sight. As much as the positive words are key for positive results, negative words often lead to _____ results.

Life Application

1. Are you having total faith in God to accomplish your vision?

2. Has your vision been tested and has it discouraged you sometimes?

3. What is your reaction when you are discouraged? Do you exhibit patience? What should be your reaction?

4. What are the current key challenges you are facing to accomplish your vision?

5. What is your attitude toward overcoming the mountains in your life?

7 Leadership and Servanthood: Step VI, Part I

The Seven Steps

Step 1: Find your Purpose and Catch the Vision
Step 2: Decide to Act and Write the Vision
Step 3: Build a Team to Accomplish the Vision
Step 4: Manage the Team & Foster Innovation
Step 5: Believe in the Vision
Step 6: Run with the Vision
Step 7: Hang on to the Vision

"Leadership is a potent combination of strategy and character. But if you must be without one, be without the strategy."
-- General H. Norman Schwarzkopf

"Leadership cannot really be taught. It can only be learned."
-- Harold S. Geneen

The typical way of looking at leadership is a triangle with the leader at the top. This fits well with the definition of leadership focusing on obtaining followers. Some people have the notion that as a leader you have to exercise authority over people all the time. That is not true. Jesus once said to his disciples "You know that those who are considered rulers of gentiles lord it over them, and their great ones exercise authority over them. Yet it shall not be so among you; but whoever desires to become great among you, let him be your servant."[48] One can become an effective leader when you are just serving others leading them down the path to success. You need to see what the team members around you need and help them to meet that need so they can run with the vision.

Once I was in a meeting with 20 leaders in the same room. Someone brought a tray with coffee and left it on a side table. One leader in the room got up and served coffee to all 20 people in the room. This really impacted my life as I witnessed servant hood in action. He built relationships with 19 other people by serving them coffee, while the rest of us may be only connected with a handful of people during the entire time. The point is that by serving people you can build strong relationships, which all leaders need to be effective at. This will help you to work through others to accomplish the vision.

The biblical way of defining leadership is a triangle upside down, where the leader is at the bottom serving others and facilitating and being the catalyst in the team to accomplish the vision. Two of Jesus' followers, James and John, during a private discussion, were vying for top leadership positions alongside Jesus. Jesus

---

48. Matthew 20:25-26

asked them if they were willing to pay the price. He went on to tell them: "Yet it shall not be so among you; but whoever desires to become great among you shall be your servant. And whoever of you desires to be first shall be slave of all. For even the Son of Man did not come to be served but to serve, and to give his life a ransom for many."[49] He was really saying that true greatness comes from serving others.

It is said that anyone who met Mother Teresa felt that she made him or her feel as if he/she was the most important person in the whole world. There is a lesson in servant leadership from Mother Teresa. If you want to be a servant leader, have the mindset to serve others and most of all, treat everyone with all due respect. A simple way of accomplishing this is to focus on others' success and helping them accomplish it. You should be a model servant leader so you can raise many servant leaders to change the world.

I have met many successful leaders in government, schools, business and the ministry. The common thread I see in most of them is humility. The word humble comes from the word humus, which means earth. It has the connotation of not being proud or haughty, nor arrogant or assertive. We call people who are humble "down to earth."

> *God resists the proud, but gives grace to the humble.*
> *-- James 4:6*

---

49. Matthew 20:28

I took my first job as a software salesman after graduating from engineering school. In my first year, I met the CEO of a large company. I was nervous, but it is amazing how good leaders make you feel very comfortable when you talk to them. I was also amazed how after the meeting he walked to the door, opened it for me and walked with me to the reception area and shook my hand as he bid me goodbye. Peter and Paul, who were leaders of the early Christian movement, often introduced themselves as fellow servants and made it clear that they were privileged to be in leadership positions, not deserving because of any superior skills or intellect. Peter often pointed out to his fellow leaders the importance of a servant attitude and humility in positions of leadership when he said the following, "...serving as overseers, not by compulsion but willingly, not for dishonest gain but eagerly; nor as being lords over those entrusted to you, but being examples."[50]

Jesus treated his disciples as equals – Leaders need to do the same. In fact, he was ready to serve. John the Baptist baptized him, though John felt Jesus should baptize him. He even washed the disciples' feet to show his ultimate servanthood. Great leaders treat team members as equals. One case in point is Alexander the Great, who fought the battle with his army, knew his soldiers on a first name basis and even shared daily meals with them.

You should develop leaders around you rather than followers. John Maxwell asserts that if you only develop followers you add to the vision, whereas if you develop leaders, you multiply the vision. Followers tend to wait for the leader's instruction and are less self-motivated. On the

---

50. 1 Peter 5:3

Chapter 7: Leadership and Servanthood: Step VI, Part I

other hand, if you develop leaders around you they will not wait for instruction, but will be proactive, think on their own, solve problems, and take responsibility. This will accelerate the accomplishment of the vision. Servant leaders are able to effectively build lasting relationships and develop leaders around them.

> *President Abraham Lincoln spent 75% of his time meeting with people.*

President Abraham Lincoln is another fine example of this line of thinking. He had an open door policy; and was willing to meet with people who did not have an appointment. Lincoln realized that people were a major source of information and to be a good leader, he had to stay close to them.

Someone once asked me if humility and confidence go hand in hand. I said yes, it does. Webster's dictionary defines confidence as faith or belief that one will act in a right, proper, or effective way or the quality or state of being certain. Although we have used Jesus in several examples throughout this book, His ability to model humility and confidence may be the most powerful example of all. He often found himself surrounded by thousands of needy people who expected Him to be the answer to their problems. In each case, He and His "team" confidently served their community and brought solutions that helped transform their lives.[51] If you intend yourself to be a great leader some day, do not overlook the importance of servanthood and

---

51. Matthew 14:15-21

humble confidence. The ultimate model for leadership is Jesus Christ and He taught us to be servant leaders.

> "A leader is a confident servant."
> -- Myles Munroe

Leadership and Servanthood

Summary
Principles

Jesus   modeled   _____ leadership.

Life
Application

1. Do you follow the Biblical style of leadership (a triangle upside down)?

2. List actions you can take to show humility or servanthood in your leadership role?

Chapter

8 Leadership and Communication: Step VI, Part II

The Seven Steps

Step 1: Find your Purpose and Catch the Vision
Step 2: Decide to Act and Write the Vision
Step 3: Build a Team to Accomplish the Vision
Step 4: Manage the Team & Foster Innovation
Step 5: Believe in the Vision
Step 6: Run with the Vision
Step 7: Hang on to the Vision

To begin with, a leader must be an effective communicator. Most of us play leadership roles in different settings; at home, church, in our companies, in social circles, or in our schools. Communication is a key quality for a leader to accomplish his or her goals. A person can be courageous and have a wonderful vision, but if they cannot communicate their goals to the team, then there can be no successful leadership.

I would like to share an example of an experiment conducted at my business school about how messages are interpreted. There was a class of 20-30 students and the first student was given a sheet of paper with some information on it. He was supposed to read it and then tell his neighbor about the contents of the information he read. His neighbor was supposed to tell another student and so on until the last student heard the information. The last student was supposed to share the information with the class. Amazingly, there was a total disconnect between what the last student said and the contents on the sheet of paper. Once you recognize that there is a lot of misinterpretation, then you will strive to communicate more clearly to avoid any misunderstanding and misinterpretation.

Here is another excellent example how communication can be easily distorted.

To: Deputy Department heads

By order of the General Manager on Friday at 5p.m., Halley's Comet will appear above the area outside the building. This rare phenomenon occurs only once every 76 years. In case of rain, we will not be able to see anything, so assemble the employees in the auditorium and I will show them a film on it.

From: Deputy Departmental Heads
To: Superintendent

By the order of the General Manager, at 5 p.m. on Friday, the phenomenal Halley's Comet will appear in the auditorium. In case of rain in the area outside the building, the General Manager will give another order, something, which occurs only once every 76 years.

From: Superintendent
To: Foreman

On Friday at 5 p.m., the General Manager will appear in the auditorium with Halley's Comet, something that happens every 76 years. But if it rains, the General Manager will order the comet into the area outside the building.

From: Foreman
To: Team Leader

When it rains on Friday at 5 p.m., the phenomenal 76-year-old Bill Halley, accompanied by his comets, will drive the General Manager through the area outside the building into the auditorium.[52]

---

52. Funtoosh.com,
http://www.funtoosh.com/dj.php?details=OFH~69

> *"The reason we have two ears and one mouth is that we may listen more and speak less."*
> *-- Zino, Greek Philosopher*

Steps for Effective Communication

Step 1. Communicate by listening. Listening is an important aspect of communication. When you listen to others, you express your respect for their views and their perspective. "Let every man be swift to hear, slow to speak and slow to wrath."[53] Churchill may end up being my top quote provider, but I enjoyed his comment: "It takes courage to stand up and speak. It takes more courage to sit down and listen."[54] Jim Collins, author of *'Good to Great'*, learned from John Gardner that we should not spend more time being interesting, but invest more time being interested.[55]

Step 2. Communicate with clarity. When leading, one needs to communicate with clarity so the team can easily understand what is being said. When you communicate you should keep your message short and simple and repeat key points. Habakkuk, a prophet in ancient Israel, proclaimed to the people, "Write the vision and make it plain on tablets, that he may run who reads it." [56]

---

53. James 1:19
54. Betterworld.net, http://www.betterworld.net/quotes/courage-quotes.htm
55. *My Golden Rule* (Business 2.0 December 2005), 109
56. Habakkuk 2:2

The tablets of stone they used were not very big forcing them to be concise. Following their lead you too should learn to keep your messages succinct. To communicate with clarity, it is a good idea to write it down and share it with the team. This will help the team to clearly understand the message. John Wesley, founder of the Methodist movement, apparently shared his messages with his maid and made sure that she understood clearly before he shared his message in public. He wanted to communicate with clarity so that even laymen could understand him clearly. Jesus Christ communicated using parables or short stories that helped people to understand His principles and remember them.

> *"Leaders inspire people with clear visions of how things can be done better. Some managers, on the other hand, muddle things with pointless complexity and details."*
> *-- Jack Welch*

Step 3. Allow for reaction time. When you communicate, you should always ask for feedback and keep it as a dialogue, rather than a monologue. Nehemiah said to the people whom he was motivating to help rebuild the wall of Jerusalem, "Come and let us build the wall of Jerusalem, that we may no longer be a reproach."[57] Then he

57. Nehemiah 2:17

actually waited for a reaction from the audience. When the people said, "Let us rise up and build!"[58] Nehemiah kicked-off the project to rebuild the wall.

Step 4. Communicate with confidence. Your personal conviction and commitment to the vision will be projected effectively when you are communicating confidently with your team. Martin Luther King, starting each eloquent paragraph of his amazing speech with "I have a dream..." epitomizes this sense of conviction.[59]

Step 5. Communicate with empathy. To communicate effectively, you need to understand the perspective of the team and know how they feel about their place in the grand scheme of things. If it is clear to them that you are aware of these feelings and acknowledge the validity of them, you will have done your job. Better yet, you will discover that if you are able to find solutions to resolve issues that touch the core of those who are following the vision, their commitment to the vision will grow and you will have become a rare leader, indeed.

Step 6. Communicate with love and compassion. When you speak with love and compassion, you improve the earning of a heartfelt commitment from every team member. "A soft answer

---

58. Nehemiah 2:18
59. Douglass Archives of American Public Address (http://douglass.speech.nwu.edu) on May 26, 1999. Prepared by D. Oetting (http://nonce.com/oetting)

turns away wrath, but a harsh word stirs up anger."[60] A sincere concern for your team will go a long way to create the synergy to succeed.

Step 7. Communicate with sincerity. Sincerity can be interpreted in more than one way. Certainly people can sense hesitance in a leader who may not have the purest of motives. They will be far less inclined to follow a leader who telegraphs doubts about a strategy or goal. If a leader communicates sincere confidence and conviction, then he or she will be more successful than the leader who communicates false bravado or who attempts to lead by trickery or deceit.

For successful leadership, there must be successful communication. In addition, leadership must be sincere if it is to be trusted. People will follow a trusted leader in the pursuit of a clearly defined and attainable goal. Communication is a key for effective leadership and you should develop your communication skills by applying these principles.

---

60. Proverbs 15:1

Leadership and Communication

Summary Principles

As a leader, the seven means of improving your communication include:

01) _____

02) _____

03) _____

04) _____

05) _____

06) _____

07) _____

Life Application

1. Which principles of communication are you applying currently?

2. Which principles of communication do you need to start applying from this point forward?

3. Set goals for you to start applying the principles of communication listed in #2 above. Have a target date to start applying those communication principles.

9 Perseverance: Step VII

The Seven Steps

Step 1: Find your Purpose and Catch the Vision
Step 2: Decide to Act and Write the Vision
Step 3: Build a Team to Accomplish the Vision
Step 4: Manage the Team & Foster Innovation
Step 5: Believe in the Vision
Step 6: Run with the Vision
Step 7: Hang on to the Vision

"Energy and persistence conquer all things."
--Benjamin Franklin

"By perseverance the snail reached the ark."
--Charles Haddon Spurgeon

"Nothing in the world can take the place of persistence. Talent will not; nothing is more common than unsuccessful men with talent. Genius will not; unrewarded genius is almost a proverb. Education will not; the world is full of educated derelicts. Persistence and determination alone are omnipotent. The slogan 'Press On' has solved and always will solve the problems of the human race."
--Calvin Coolidge

You will find that in the final stages of seeing the vision fulfilled, perseverance is the one key ingredient that alone will see you through to the end. The vision will be tested in every phase and the leader needs to show perseverance to continue to run with it. "Forgetting those things which are behind and reaching forward to those things which are ahead, I press toward the goal for the upward call of God in Christ Jesus."[61] These are the words of Paul who pressed on for the purpose, which Jesus Christ lay hold of him and kept focus on the goal and worked tirelessly to achieve it. Sometimes visionaries seem foolish to others around them who do not understand their vision and the reason for their perseverance.

Navigating Through Failure and Change

"Success is going from failure to failure without losing enthusiasm."
--Winston Churchill

---

61. Phillippians 3:14

It goes without saying that along the journey you will encounter failure along with success. That is to say, as you continue along the path of accomplishing your vision, some activities will successfully bring you closer to your goals while others may fail in moving you in the right direction. At Mindbrook, though the initial vision was to focus on enterprise management software, we found greener pastures in the compliance management arena. Perhaps the failure here was not listening intently enough to the prospective customers' needs and therefore we were not able to offer a solution that was compelling enough for them to embrace and implement. This did not discourage us from continuing to run with the vision, but allowed us to redirect our focus on providing software solutions in the more compelling compliance management space. The primary focus of visionaries should be on the vision. There will be challenges along the way. You should attack the challenges and fight against discouragement. As you hold steadfast and navigate through your challenges, slowly but surely your vision will take shape and begin to be accomplished.

In addition to fighting challenges within, you will find that many do not understand why visionaries persevere so valiantly. For example, Edison is quoted as saying it would take a matter of a few weeks to invent the lightbulb. In reality, it would take him almost two years of failed attempts, new discoveries and prototypes before he would find success. It is said that he tried over 6,000 different carbonized plant fibers, looking for a carbon filament for his light bulb. Edison's friends must have wondered, after over 6,000 tests, whether his filaments would actually produce the first practical light bulb.[62]

A local pastor who was trying to reach out to a family in his community. He used to knock at their door every Saturday morning, rain or shine. They never opened the door, yet over the course of two years he persistently called on them every Saturday. One Saturday as he came to their home, the neighbors told him that they had moved and hadn't told them where they were going. As the pastor was praying, he received divine direction to their new location. Sure enough, he went to that place and there they were. They could not believe that the pastor had found them, as they had not told anyone where they were moving. They immediately opened the door and upon hearing the gospel message decided to dedicate their lives to the Lord Jesus Christ. Now that is perseverance.

Do you give up too easily? Have you developed perseverance in what you have been assigned to do? Be patient and do not take your eyes off the vision. The vision is for an appointed time and it will come to pass. More often than not, it takes years for one to accomplish their vision. It can happen sooner than you expect, but you need to be willing to hang on to the vision until it is fulfilled.

---

62. Graceproducts.com,
http://www.graceproducts.com/edison/life.html

Chapter 9: Perseverance: Step VII

Perseverance

Summary Principles

The vision will be tested in every phase and the leader needs to show _____ to continue to run with the vision.

Life Application

1. What is the longest period of time you have waited for a dream or desire to become a reality?

2. What emotions did you experience throughout the wait?

3. Would changing your attitude toward the wait have altered the emotions you experienced?

4. In waiting for your current vision to become reality, what attitude(s) and practice(s) could engender positive perseverance for you?

10 Transforming Communities

I once heard a preacher talking about some of the major issues in the world today and I was quite frankly, completely "blown away". He listed the following:

- *11 million children die each year*
- *15 million women die each year giving birth*
- *900 million women in the world cannot read or write*
- *1.5 billion people around the world do not have clean drinking water*
- *Tens of millions still do not have electricity*

Despite unprecedented economic growth occurring in various developing countries, most of the people living there find that their plight remains the same. At the same time, industrialized nations and their communities continue to have their own overwhelming domestic issues despite the prevailing belief of "how far we have progressed." It is my strong conviction that whether it is a personal or corporate vision, a great leader must come to terms with the fact that they have a responsibility to integrate into the vision the transformation of their community. In fact, a vital part of my personal vision is to see this become a reality in communities around the world.

Model for Community Transformation

In order for a community to be transformed, it has to be transformed spiritually, socially and economically.

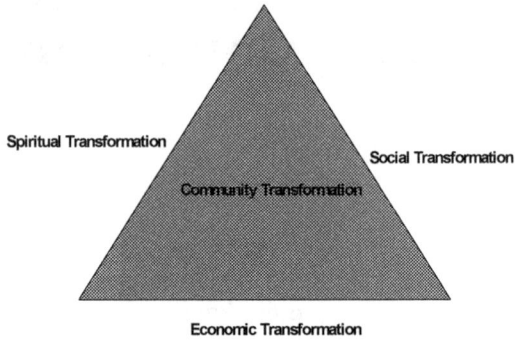

Spiritual Transformation

Social Transformation

Community Transformation

Economic Transformation

The way you need to approach this is to first find out the needs in the community. You can talk to community leaders like the mayor, the police chief and the school superintendent and ask them about the concerns of their community. Once you find the needs, you can address them. Successful community transformation cannot be accomplished alone or by one organization. It has to be a united effort between government, schools, churches, businesses and faith-based or other non-profit organizations.

Currently, I am personally involved in a movement to transform the community of a small city in the Silicon Valley. In fact, we talked to the mayor, police chief and school superintendent. Each of them confirmed that elementary school kids need greater guidance and support to overcome the common pressures faced by this generation. We have already developed an after-school program, which has grown from 40 to 120 kids in three short months. Moving forward, we have planned more initiatives and we have five different organizations partnering with us.

How Can My Vision be Involved?

As you are venturing out and executing your vision, you should keep your community in mind. You should look for ways your organization can be a blessing to the community and also collaborate with other organizations on these types of projects. If your organization is already doing that, great! If not, I encourage you to initiate the effort in finding a way to serve your community through your vision. Global companies can consider adopting a community in a developing country (like IBM, which has a development center in Bangalore, India) in order to help transform that community. As a company works within its community, it may find unanticipated benefits. The goodwill and public relations alone could save millions of dollars in the marketing communications budget!

As well as an increased awareness within the corporate world of their social responsibility, there is a global trend toward social entrepreneurship. One good definition of social entrepreneurship can be found in the mission statement of Pura Vida Coffee: "To create good by using capitalism to empower producers, motivate consumers, inspire business leaders, and ultimately serve the poor."[63]

Another interesting economic transformation concept is micro-credit. Mohammad Yunus, founder of Grameen Bank in Bangladesh

---

63. Puravidacoffeee.com,
http://www.puravidacoffee.com/work/work_body.asp

recently won the Nobel Peace Prize for his pioneering use of micro-credit -- small loans averaging $200 -- to lift millions out of poverty.[64]

If leaders are inspired to integrate a goal for community transformation within their vision, we will be well on our way to solving the spiritual, social and economic problems throughout the nations of the world. Consider the community transformation model presented in this chapter, remembering that successful transformation results from the efforts of many.

---

64. Gdrc.org,
http://www.gdrc.org/icm/grameen-info.html

Transforming Communities

**Summary
Principles**

```
                    /\
                   /  \
                  /    \
_____ /      \ _____
                /        \
               /  Community Transformation  \
              /            \
             /_____\

              _____
```

**Life
Application**

1. What are your perceptions of your community's needs? List 2-3.

2. Who among your community leaders is most likely to know and explain its needs as perceived by the members of the community? List them.

3. Choose the top 4 leaders from your list. How can you contact each of these four? Can you bring them all together for a single initial meeting?

For Future Follow-up...

1. What community needs did your 4 leaders put forth?

2. How well do your perceptions match the leaders' perceptions?

3. Which of these needs can your organization positively impact?

4. Rewrite your vision statement to include the goal to positively impact your community in this way.

5. Now, who else can you partner with? Build your team keeping the community transformation model in mind.

Conclusion

Final words from a man who is still running with his vision

As I am sitting here in my home in San Jose with my friend and writing coach Frank, I look back to my opening statements. I really hope to have accomplished just one thing, which is to have inspired you to find your purpose and God given vision and decide to take action.

Not many act...

I trust you will be different.

To know your true purpose from God you need to have a relationship with God. I am not talking about joining a church or finding religion.

Would you pray with me? Lord Jesus, I repent of my sins, I ask you to come into my heart, I make you my LORD and Savior. Please guide me to accomplish my true purpose.

If you prayed that prayer, I believe that you have been "born again". I encourage you to attend a good Bible-based Church.

We would love to hear from you!

To contact us, write to:

- Cyril & Jemima Rayan
  P.O Box 23733
  San Jose, CA - 95153-3733

- For more information, please visit our web sites
- http://www.pottersministries.org
  http://www.mindbrook.com

or send me email to either

- Cyril@pottersministries.org
  Cyril@mindbrook.com

About the Author

Cyril Rayan is Founder, President & CEO of Mindbrook Inc. a start-up software company in the compliance management space. He has fourteen years experience in the semiconductor/software industry. He has more than 9 years experience in International marketing and sales. In his last position he was a worldwide product manager at ZiLOG, Inc.

He is an Associate Professor at Bethany University where he teaches marketing, leadership and management. He is an adjunct professor at William Jessup University. He is a Co-founder of the Potter's Ministries which is a Christian non-profit organization involved in community transformation. He is also

Co-founder of the Christian open development network, which is an open source movement in the Christian community for software projects.

Cyril has a passion for studying and speaking on leadership. He holds a master's degree in Electrical Engineering and an MBA from Santa Clara University. For more information visit his leadership blog http://www.cyrilrayan.com

Cyril and his wife, Jemima, travel together as seminar speakers and are the proud parents of two children, Hannah and Joshua.

'Moving From Vision to Reality' Seminar

There are several managers, but we see very few leaders. This seminar will help develop leaders in your organization.

Topics Covered:
- Leadership, Purpose & Vision
- Leadership Qualities
- Leadership and Management
- Leaders are servants

Learn
- To align with the vision
- To recognize your purpose in accomplishing the vision
- To be a servant leader
- To lead and manage effectively

Logistics: This 3 hour seminar can be organized at your organization or a neutral site. Email: Cyril@mindbrook.com for more information.

Comments about the Seminar: Cyril is living "From Vision to Reality" in his business and the ministry he co-founded; that's what makes this seminar very effective. The seminar definitely helped to develop servant leaders at our organization and leaders came forward and accepted responsibilities. I now have a team of leaders around me who are supporting me. I strongly recommend this seminar.

John Matthew
A non-profit organization, NY

Create Thought Leadership for your Company

Books deliver instant credibility to the author. Having an MBA or PhD is great, however, putting the word "author" in front of your name is similar to using the letters PHD or MBA. You are no long Michael Green, you are "Author Michael Green."

Books give you a platform to stand on. They help you to:

- Demonstrate your thought leadership
- Generate leads

Books deliver increased revenue, particularly indirect revenue

- A typical consultant will make 3x in indirect revenue for every dollar they make on book sales

Books are better than a business card. They are:

- More powerful than white papers
- An item that makes it to the book shelf vs. the circular file
- The best tschocke you can give at a conference

Why wait to write your book?

Check out other companies that have built credibility by writing and publishing a book through Happy About

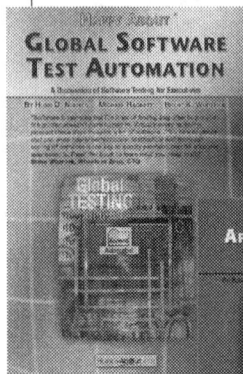

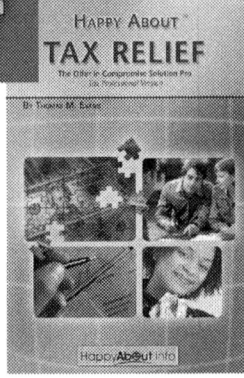

Contact Happy About at 408-257-3000 or go to http://happyabout.info.

Purchase at http://happyabout.info or at other
online and physical bookstores.

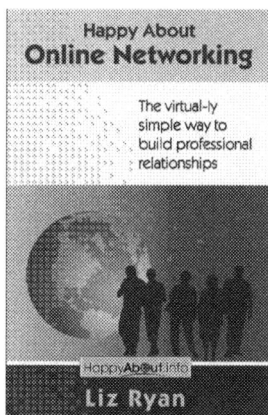

Happy About
Online Networking

The virtual-ly
simple way to
build professional
relationships

HappyAbout.info

Liz Ryan

*Learn the tricks and
techniques you need to
be effective!*

This book outlines the
tools, methods, and
protocols of creating and
cultivating an online
network for global reach,
business and personal
support, and professional
success.

Paperback:$19.95 132pgs
eBook:$ 11.95 132pgs

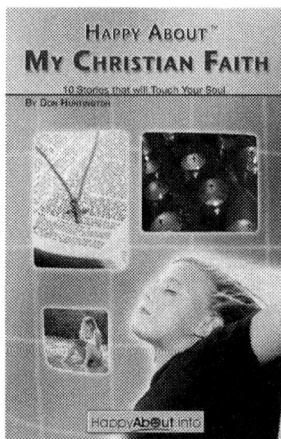

HAPPY ABOUT
MY CHRISTIAN FAITH

10 Stories that will Touch Your Soul
By Don Huntington

HappyAbout.info

**Read this book if you
want to laugh, cry, and
be inspired.**

Many of us wish that we
could lead lives of
service, and would prefer
one day to leave the
world a better place
because we were in it
while others are on a
quest for personal
redemption.

Paperback: $16.95 184pgs
eBook: $11.95 172pgs

www.ingramcontent.com/pod-product-compliance
Lightning Source LLC
Chambersburg PA
CBHW060548100426
42742CB00013B/2488